Contents

Welcome to France

France is a wonderful place to visit and there is plenty to discover about this incredible country. Perhaps you like reading about historic battles, amazing art and wonderful food. Whatever your reason for picking up this book, you will discover that the story of France is thrilling. France has a long history, a beautiful landscape and countless fascinating people.

Tips to get you started

• Look at the pictures

This book has lots of great photos. Flip through and find the pictures you like the best. This is a quick way to get an idea of what this book is all about. Read the captions to learn even more about the photos.

• Use the glossary

As you read this book, you may notice that some words appear in **bold** print. Look up bold words in the glossary at the back of the book. The glossary will help you learn what they mean.

• Use the index

If you are looking for a certain fact about France, then you might want to go to the index, also at the back of the book. The index contains a list of all the subjects covered in the book.

world tour
France

CHRISTOPHER MITTEN

www.raintreepublishers.co.uk
Visit our website to find out more information about Raintree books.

To order:
☎ Phone 44 (0) 1865 888112
🗎 Send a fax to 44 (0) 1865 314091
🖥 Visit the Raintree Bookshop at **www.raintreepublishers.co.uk** to browse our catalogue and order online.

First published in Great Britain by Raintree Publishers, Halley Court, Jordan Hill, Oxford, OX2 8EJ, part of Harcourt Education.
Raintree is a registered trademark of Harcourt Education Ltd.

© Harcourt Education Ltd 2003
The moral right of the proprieter has been asserted.

All rights reserved. No part of this publication may be reproduced, stored in a retrieval system, or transmitted in any form or by any means, electronic, mechanical, photocopying, recording, or otherwise, without either the prior written permission of the publishers or a licence permitting restricted copying in the United Kingdom issued by the Copyright Licensing Agency Ltd, 90 Tottenham Court Road, London W1T 4LP (www.cla.co.uk).

Editorial: Sally Knowles
Cover Design: Peter Bailey and Michelle Lisseter
Production: Jonathan Smith

Printed and bound in China and Hong Kong by South China Printing Company

ISBN 1 844 21305 6
07 06 05 04 03
10 9 8 7 6 5 4 3 2 1

British Library Cataloguing in Publication Data
Mitten, Christopher
France. - (World tour)
944
A full catalogue for this book is available from the British Library

Acknowledgements
The publishers would like to thank the following for permission to reproduce photographs
p. **1a** ©Richard T. Nowitz; p. **1b** ©eStock; p. **1c** ©SuperStock; p. **3a** ©Becky Luigart-Stayner/CORBIS; p. **3b** ©Gail Mooney/CORBIS; p. **5** ©SuperStock; p. **6** ©AKG Berlin/SuperStock; p. **7** ©Charles Graham/eStock; p. **8** ©AFP/CORBIS; p. **13a** ©Adam Woolfitt/CORBIS; p. **13b** ©SIME/ eStock; p. **14** ©Dalmasso/ImageState; p. **15** ©Patrick Ingrand/Getty Images; p. **16** ©Steve Vidler/ SuperStock; p. **17** ©eStock; p. **19** ©Murat Ayranci/ SuperStock; p. **21** ©Adam Woolfitt/CORBIS; p. **22** ©Archivo Iconografico/CORBIS; p. **23** ©Charles E. Rotkin/CORBIS; p. **24** ©Gail Mooney/ CORBIS p. **25** ©AFP/ CORBIS; p. **27a** ©eStock; p. **27b** Marc Garanger/CORBIS; p. **28** ©Beryl Goldberg; p. **29** ©AFP/CORBIS; p. **31a** ©Reuters NewMedia Inc/CORBIS; p. **31b** ©Owen Franken/ CORBIS; p. **33** ©David Warren/ SuperStock; p. **34** ©Owen Franken/ CORBIS; p. **35** ©Michael Boys/ CORBIS; p. **37** ©Sandro Vannini/CORBIS; p. **39** ©Brian Leatart/FoodPix; p. **40** ©AFP/ CORBIS; p. **41** ©Anne B. Keiser/ SuperStock; p. **42** ©Steve Vidler/ SuperStock; p. **43b** ©Gail Mooney/CORBIS; p. **43c** ©European Central Bank, Frankfurt, p. **44a** ©Rufus F Folkks/CORBIS; p. **44b,c** ©Bettmann/ CORBIS.

Cover photography: Background: Getty Images/Taxi. Foreground: Getty Images/Stone/Howard Kingsnorth

Every effort has been made to contact copyright holders of any material reproduced in this book. Any omissions will be rectified in subsequent printing if notice is given to the publishers.

▲ VINEYARDS IN MARANGES, FRANCE
France is known for its wonderful wines. Some of the most beautiful grape vineyards are found at Maranges. As you walk through the hills, you can smell the grapes.

France's past

The history of France is filled with great stories – of wars and battles, kings, queens, an emperor and a **revolution**.

Ancient history

A Celtic people called the Gauls were the earliest known **ancestors** of modern-day French people. The Gauls arrived between 1500 and 800 BC. By AD 400, tribes from the east began raiding Gaul. The most powerful tribe was the Franks. They quickly took over. The region has been known as France ever since.

In the centuries that followed, five important **dynasties** ruled France. The last, and most important, was the Bourbon dynasty. The first Bourbon king was Henry of Navarre. He ended centuries of religious wars between Catholics and Protestants. King Louis XIV (XIV means 'fourteenth') was the most important Bourbon king. He was known as the Sun King. He ruled from 1643 to 1715. During his reign, France enjoyed its Golden Age and became the greatest power in Europe.

◀ PLACE DES PYRAMIDES
This statue of Joan of Arc is in Paris. At the age of seventeen, Joan of Arc led the French army to victory against the English in the 1400s. She was captured and burnt at the stake in 1431.

AN ARTIST'S DREAM SPOT ▶
Claude Monet was a famous
French artist known for his
paintings of this garden in
Giverny, France. It is among
the most beautiful gardens
in the world.

The French Revolution and Napoleon

In 1789, the French Revolution began. The French
people were angry because they were poor and were
tired of supporting a king and his very expensive court.

They created a new government. This led to a
period of political violence known as the Terror.
Thousands were executed on the **guillotine** – including
the king and queen. Then a brilliant young general
called Napoleon Bonaparte took control and ended the
Terror. In 1804, he declared himself the country's
emperor. Napoleon conquered most of Europe. He was
defeated at the battle of Waterloo in 1815.

France in the 19th century

After Napoleon, France struggled to find a **stable** form
of government. In 1871, **democracy** was restored.
During this period, many changes took place. Huge
factories, railways and banks were built all over France.
People moved to the city to work in factories rather
than on farms. French literature and art began to explore
Realism and **Impressionism**, with thrilling results.

◀ **MODERN POLITICS**
Jacques Chirac, current
president of France, gives a
speech to farmers in the
eastern village of Pomacle.

The World Wars

Sadly, the good times at the end of the 19th century did not last for long. In 1914, Europe plunged into troubled times that began with The Great War, or World War I.

This war lasted from 1914 to 1918. France, Britain, the USA and Russia formed an **alliance** on one side. The Austrians and Germans were on the other. World War I was bloodier than any war had ever been. More than 1 million French soldiers died and over 4 million were wounded.

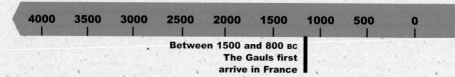

BC | 4000 | 3500 | 3000 | 2500 | 2000 | 1500 | 1000 | 500 | 0

Between 1500 and 800 BC
The Gauls first
arrive in France

France and its allies won the war, but Europe was badly affected. By the mid-1930s, France experienced the effects of a worldwide **economic depression**. In Germany, the **Nazi** leader Adolf Hitler rose to power. He wanted revenge for Germany's defeat and a solution to the depression. Hitler blamed Europe's Jews for Germany's problems. In 1939, Hitler's **invasion** of Poland began World War II.

As in World War I, France allied with Great Britain, Russia and the USA but Germany invaded France in 1940. During the war, the Nazis killed more than 6 million European Jews. About 75,000 of these victims were French.

Recent times

When World War II ended, France formed a democratic government. In the years after the war, France faced a major question: what should happen to its **foreign colonies** in the Far East and Africa, such as Vietnam, Algeria and Senegal? By the 1970s, France's colonies had become **independent**. Now France is one of the most stable and prosperous nations in the world, its future looks even brighter.

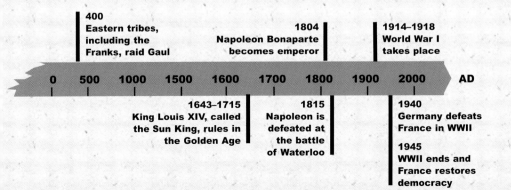

400
Eastern tribes, including the Franks, raid Gaul

1804
Napoleon Bonaparte becomes emperor

1914–1918
World War I takes place

0   500   1000   1500   1600   1700   1800   1900   2000   AD

1643–1715
King Louis XIV, called the Sun King, rules in the Golden Age

1815
Napoleon is defeated at the battle of Waterloo

1940
Germany defeats France in WWII

1945
WWII ends and France restores democracy

A look at France's geography

If you are looking for a place that has lots of different types of scenery, then France is perfect. Its mountain ranges contain some of Europe's highest peaks. Its coastlines are popular with the rich and famous. Inland, you will find **fertile** farmland. There is almost every landscape a traveller could want to see.

Land

There are three main mountain ranges in France. The Pyrenées lie to the south and separate France from Spain. To the east, the Jura Mountains stand along the border with Switzerland. South-east of the Jura are the Alps. Mont Blanc, the tallest mountain in France, is part of the Alps and stands 4807 metres high.

The rest of France is mostly flat. Much of this land is used for farming. Over 90 per cent of French land is fertile. This means that there are lots of **nutrients** in the soil, so plants can grow well. In the north, the plains are wet and rich with **vegetation**. In the middle, the land is drier and less fertile, although there are still many farms in this part of the country. In south-west France the weather is wetter and the land is perfect for growing grapes to make wine.

FRANCE'S SIZE ▶
France is the largest country in western Europe. Its total area is 543,965 sq km (210,026 sq miles). France borders Belgium, Luxembourg, Germany, Switzerland, Italy, Monaco, Andorra and Spain. The United Kingdom lies across the English Channel.

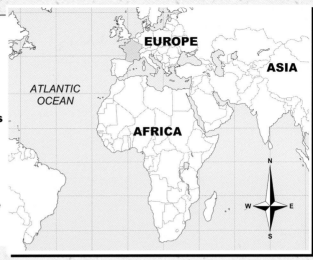

FRANCE

- ★ National capital
- ● Major city
- — River

0 50 100 Kilometres
0   50   100 Miles

Water

Four main bodies of water surround France. To the west lies the Bay of Biscay, which is part of the Atlantic Ocean. To the south lies the Mediterranean Sea. To the north is the English Channel, and at the north-east tip is the North Sea. Altogether, France has just over 3200 kilometres (2000 miles) of coastline.

Rivers play a major role in France's geography. France's longest river is the Loire. It stretches for about 1020 kilometres (635 miles). The Rhine marks the border between France and Germany. Another major river in France is the Rhône. This river runs south from the Alps to the Mediterranean. The famous Seine runs through Paris, France's capital.

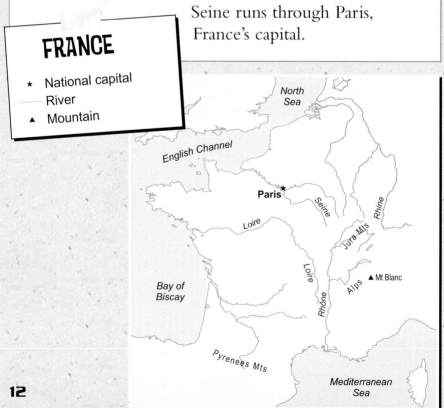

FRANCE

★ National capital
— River
▲ Mountain

North Sea

English Channel

Paris ★

Seine

Rhine

Loire

Jura Mts

Loire

Alps ▲ Mt Blanc

Bay of Biscay

Rhône

Pyrenees Mts

Mediterranean Sea

▲ LOIRE RIVER
Did you know that the Loire is the last wild river in western Europe? It flows naturally and has no artificial structures such as dams.

ON THE BEACH IN CORSICA ▶
Going down to the beach takes on a whole new meaning in Corsica. This lovely French island is home to some of the most magnificent ocean views.

◀ **WALKING IN THE ALPS**
Mont Blanc, which means
'White Mountain', is the highest
peak in France. Wrap up warm
because it can be very cold in
the Alps.

Climate

France lies halfway between the **equator** and the North Pole. It has a **temperate climate**, which means that the temperatures are moderate. Of course, the climate is not the same all over France, it varies from place to place.

The coldest place in France is the area around Mont Blanc in the Alps. It is surrounded by large glaciers – permanent fields of ice.

The warmest place is France's Mediterranean coast. The temperature can reach as high as 28°C in the summer, when hundreds of people come to enjoy the beaches. In the winter, it stays at about 12°C.

Paris, the capital of France, is a little cooler than the south coast. In the winter, the average high is 4°C. In the summer, temperatures often reach 24°C.

▲ WINE HARVEST
This man from Vaucluse, France, knows that harvesting grapes is important in wine country. France has the perfect climate to grow first-class grapes.

Paris: snapshot of a big city

▲ **A STROLL IN PARIS**
It is hard to walk down this Parisian street without taking
your eyes off the Eiffel Tower. This world-famous monument
has a must-see view of the city.

There is always something to do or to see in Paris, the capital of France. Paris is split in two by a river called the Seine. There are many bridges across the river, so it is easy to get around.

The Right Bank

You may want to begin your sightseeing at the Arc de Triomphe. It is a huge arch that sits in the middle of a busy intersection. Napoleon started building the arch to celebrate his triumph in battle. Today, the Arc de Triomphe **commemorates** France's fallen soldiers.

Next, head to the Louvre. Once a royal palace, this is one of the biggest and most famous art museums in the world. The Louvre's most famous painting is the Mona Lisa, by Leonardo da Vinci. It is kept in a heavily protected display case. If you want to see this painting, be prepared to wait as it is often surrounded by crowds.

DOWNTOWN ▶
Paris looks wonderful from the Eiffel Tower.

Across the river

Each of the many bridges across the Seine has its own charm and its own unique views. To start, head to the Left Bank across the Pont D'Arcole. It will take you to an island in the Seine called Ile de la Cité. This island is home to Paris's most famous cathedral, Notre Dame. Its construction began in 1163 and took 200 years to complete. Inside, you can see where Napoleon crowned himself emperor in 1804.

The Left Bank

Paris's Left Bank is home to the University of Paris and to the nearby Panthéon. This huge, domed building is a monument to France's great thinkers and philosophers and many of them are buried there.

To the west you will find the gardens and perfect lawns of the Jardins du Luxembourg. The Palais du Luxembourg in the gardens currently houses the French Senate and there are often lots of politicians there. There are lots of chairs and benches in the gardens – a good place to enjoy a picnic.

From the Jardins du Luxembourg you can see the top of the Eiffel Tower. This landmark was built in 1889 to commemorate the Revolution and to show off French engineering skills. The tower shocked Parisians then. They thought it was ugly but today, people love it. The view from the top of the tower is amazing.

THE LOUVRE ▶
The Louvre is one of the most famous museums in the world. It is home to the famous painting of the Mona Lisa by Leonardo da Vinci.

PARIS'S TOP-TEN CHECKLIST

If you are heading to Paris, here is a list of the top ten things to do there:

- ☐ Visit the grave of the Unknown Soldier at the Arc de Triomphe.
- ☐ Walk down the Champs Elysées.
- ☐ Look at some modern art at the futuristic Pompidou Centre.
- ☐ Go window-shopping in the fabulous Right Bank shops.
- ☐ Wander around the Louvre looking at the paintings. Make sure you see the Mona Lisa.
- ☐ Cross the famous bridges over the Seine.
- ☐ Take a tour of the cathedral of Notre Dame.
- ☐ Take a boat ride on the Seine.
- ☐ Enjoy a picnic in the Jardins du Luxembourg.
- ☐ Take the lift to the top of the Eiffel Tower and admire the view.

Four top sights

Mont Saint Michel

Mont Saint Michel is a tiny town built on an island off the north coast of France. It has one main street which winds up a hill. It is only an island for part of the day – when the tide is high. When the tide goes out, it is a little town sitting above long stretches of wet sand.

This town's most impressive building is the abbey. An abbey is a place where Christian **monks** or nuns live and worship. The abbey at Mont Saint Michel is huge, and it sits on the top of the hill. Construction of Mont Saint Michel started in AD 708. The really impressive parts were built in the 11th and 12th centuries, when the abbey church was begun.

Below the abbey, where monks still live, is the main street of Mont Saint Michel. In fact, it is the island's only street, called the Grand Rue. It is filled with shops, hotels and restaurants. There is a restaurant there called La Mere Poulard which is famous for omelettes.

The luckiest visitors can stay the night and watch the tides come in, turning a tiny town into an enchanted island.

▲ **MONT ST MICHEL**
**Above, what looks like a fairytale castle is really an abbey
– a place where Christian monks lived. Parts of this
fortress were built in 1137.**

Versailles

In 1789, revolution broke out in France. The lower and middle classes grew tired of rich people taking their money and spending it on **luxuries**. If you are curious to see some of these luxuries, make a visit to Versailles.

King Louis XIV built the royal palace of Versailles at the end of the 17th century. Inside you will find fabulous **décor**. Go and look at the Hall of Mirrors with its huge **chandeliers** or visit Louis XIV's private chapel. Then step outside to see the gardens. Versailles is famous for its perfect lawns, huge fountains and rare flowers.

▲ HALL OF MIRRORS
This room seems to go on for ever and ever. With an endless line of huge mirrors and chandeliers, the Hall of Mirrors is quite a sight.

▲ THE ROYAL PALACE
This national treasure was once home to the kings of
France. Louis XIV converted it from a hunting lodge to a
palace with gardens. Versailles is now a national museum.

Cannes

People who prefer the beach to go to Cannes, by the Mediterranean Sea. Start your visit by walking down the Boulevard de la Croisette. This is the best place to people-watch. Have a look at the designer shops and watch the yachts come in and out of the harbour.

Next, find a place on one of the beaches. You might spot one of the film stars who often stay in Cannes.

Lots of people come to Cannes in May as this is when the famous Cannes Film Festival takes place. It is very busy, with lots of shows, award ceremonies and parties. Many actors and film makers think that an award from the Cannes Film Festival is more valuable than an Oscar.

▲ EVENING IN CANNES
When you have finished spotting the rich and famous, you might want to go for a walk. There is a lot to see in Cannes.

▼ FILM FESTIVAL

Winning an award at the Cannes Film Festival is a huge honour. Actors, actresses and directors from around the world flock to Cannes each May for the festival.

Chamonix and Mont Blanc

Chamonix and Mont Blanc are in the Alps near the border with Switzerland. The mountain scenery is spectacular. A popular food in this part France is cheese fondue – you dip pieces of bread in a pot of hot melted cheese. It is an ideal snack after a long day of walking around the foothills of Mont Blanc.

The town of Chamonix is like a little Paris-in-the-mountains. There are lots of shops, restaurants and old houses on pretty streets.

Chamonix really comes alive in the winter as people come to ski on some of the best ski slopes in the world. In the summer, you can explore the many trails that wind through the mountains. The easiest way to get to some of these trails is by the cable car which will take you high into the mountains for a fantastic view of Mont Blanc, the highest peak in France. If you want to climb Mont Blanc, you will need to start training now. Only the best mountain climbers can make it to the top of this mountain.

CHAIRLIFT AT MONT BLANC ▶
You can take a chairlift up Mont Blanc. This is the highest peak in the European Alps.

▼ RIVER ARVE IN CHAMONIX
You can get your fill of French life by the river, which is lined with shops and restaurants.

Going to school in France

France has one of the best education systems in the world. French children start school at age five or six, and can leave at sixteen but most continue until they are eighteen. When students turn fifteen, they make a decision about what they want to do with their lives. Some choose vocational school, where they learn trades such as car mechanics or plumbing. Other students work to pass an exam called the Baccalauréat. They must pass this exam if they want to go to college.

About 15 per cent of students in France attend private schools. These schools are often religious.

▲ A FRENCH CLASSROOM
These French students learn many of the same subjects as you, such as maths, science and social studies.

French sports

France's number one sport is definitely football. Go to any small town in France and you are sure to find a local football ground. The French national football team won the World Cup in 1998, a feat most countries only dream about.

Cycling is another popular French sport. Each year France holds the Tour de France. It is a bicycle race through the towns and countryside that lasts for three weeks. In the cycling world, this is the most important event of the year.

The French also love tennis. Every summer they host a tennis competition called the French Open. It is one of the most important tennis tournaments in the world.

▲ BICYCLE RACING
The Tour de France is the most famous bike race in the world. Cyclists from all over the world come to France to compete in it.

From farming to factories

France has one of the strongest economies in the world. The French produce cars, medicines, wine and electronics. These industries employ millions of workers, and their products are sold all over the world.

Food production is a very important industry. Farmers grow crops and raise animals. Small factories are also involved in the food business, making a wide range of foods, such as wine, cheese, jams and biscuits. French wine is **exported** all over the world and people will pay a lot of euros for a good bottle. The euro is the currency used in France.

France's **natural resources** include wood and metals. Workers help to find these resources and prepare them for export.

Many French people work in the tourist industry. They run the hotels and restaurants that take care of tourists when they come to visit. They also work in the tourist attractions and museums, and run the public transport.

FRENCH CHEESES ▶
Wine and cheese is a
perfect combination. In
France, making cheese is
an art form. There are
about 700 types of
French cheese including
brie, camembert, port
salut and roquefort.

▲ **HARVESTING GRAPES**
Handy wicker baskets make grape collecting easier.
These grape pickers work through the day. The grapes
are used to make fine wine.

The French government

France is a democracy. That means that the people vote to elect their leaders.

France has a president, who is elected directly by the people. The president's term lasts for five years. The president works closely with the Assemblée Nationale, which makes the laws in France. There are 577 members of the Assemblée Nationale elected by the members' home provinces. They serve for five years.

France also has a senate, which has 321 members. The people do not elect these senators. Regional governments choose them. The senate does not have much power. It serves mostly to advise the national government.

France is also divided into 101 départments or districts. Each départment has its own local government. Local governments work closely with France's national government.

FRANCE'S NATIONAL FLAG

The flag has three panels — blue, white and red. The red and blue are traditional colours of Paris. The red may represent Saint Denis, the patron saint of Paris, and the blue, Saint Martin, who wore a blue coat, which he gave to a beggar (a symbol of charity). The white represents the purity of the Virgin Mary and Joan of Arc, and is the colour of royalty in France.

Religions of France

Between 80 and 88 per cent of French people are Roman Catholic. Catholics are Christians who follow the teachings of Jesus found in the New Testament of the Bible. Catholics are different from other Christians because they follow the leadership of the Pope, who lives in the Vatican City in Italy. About 2 per cent of French people are Protestants. Protestants are also Christians, but they do not follow the Pope.

About 5 to 10 per cent of the French population are Muslims. Muslims follow the teachings of Mohammed, which are found in their holy book, called the Koran. Many French Muslims are from African countries like Algeria and Tunisia, which were once French colonies.

In addition, Jews make up about 1 per cent of the French population. They follow the teachings of the Torah found in the Old Testament of the Bible.

◀ GOTHIC CHURCH
Gothic design is an old style of architecture. Chartres Cathedral follows this traditional style. There are many beautiful cathedrals all over France.

French food

French food is some of the best in the world and has influenced cooking all over the globe. You will probably have had French food at home or at a restaurant, such as French fries (*pommes frites*) or French toast (*pain d'or*).

The French make hundreds of different kinds of cheese and there are wonderful cheeses from every region of France. Brie and camembert are among the most popular.

French people often eat cheese at the end of dinner. They might start with soup. One popular soup is consommé, a clear meat broth. Another is vichyssoise, which is cold potato and leek soup. The main course often includes meat in a **gourmet** sauce, vegetables and a starchy food, such as potato or rice. The French will also definitely serve their wonderful bread, and they enjoy green salads after the main course.

French desserts include ice cream, sorbets and various mouth-watering cakes and pies. Mousse is another well-known French dessert.

◄ **FROGS' LEGS**
When they are cooked, you may not be able to tell these are frogs' legs. This tasty dish is a French speciality.

France's recipe

CHOCOLATE MOUSSE

INGREDIENTS:
320g dark chocolate
2 large eggs
2 tsp vanilla esence
500 ml double cream, heated

WARNING:
**Never cook or bake by yourself.
Always ask an adult to help you
in the kitchen.**

DIRECTIONS:
**Put the cream in a saucepan and
put on a low heat. Place the
chocolate chips, the eggs and the
vanilla in a food processor.
Mix for about half a minute.
When the cream is hot, slowly pour it into the food
processor while continuing to mix. Stop mixing when the
chocolate mixture is smooth and the chocolate chips are
perfectly blended. Next, pour the chocolate mixture into
small bowls and refrigerate. The mousse is ready to
serve as soon as it has set.**

Up close: Corsica

Corsica is the third-largest island in the Mediterranean Sea. Its area is about 8680 square kilometres (3350 square miles). It has nearly 1000 kilometres (625 miles) of beautiful, sunny coastline. The mountains in the centre of the island have snow on them.

Corsica is close to Italy and over the years, Italian kingdoms have claimed the island as their own. In 1768, Corsica was sold to the French for 40 million francs. Of course, many Corsicans were not happy about being bought and sold. There are still some people in Corsica who want independence. Many Corsicans, however, are happy to be part of France.

Corsica's claim to fame is as the birthplace of Napoleon, who became emperor of France in 1804. At the height of his power, Napoleon controlled most of western Europe.

Walking, swimming and exploring

Corsica has one of the largest national parks in Europe. It is called Parc Naturel Régional de Corse and it covers almost half the island. The park stretches from the beaches inland to Corsica's highest mountain, Monte Cinto which is about 2710 metres high. Frà Li Monti is one of the most popular walking trails through this park. It crosses several mountains and is about 160 kilometres (100 miles) long.

▲ CORSICAN CASTLE
There are plenty of castles in Corsica. This castle in Corte
makes a good photo opportunity.

Corsica's towns and villages

Corsica is an interesting place to visit because parts of it have not changed for hundreds of years. Narrow, winding streets surround ancient churches in the villages and there are fortresses looming above every settlement.

Bastia is a booming **port** town in the north of Corsica. It was built near a 16th-century fortress. Be sure to shop at the huge open-air market near the Hôtel de Ville (town hall) where you can pick up goats' cheese and olives to eat on your walk up Monte Cinto.

Corte is a city in the middle of Corsica, high in Corsica's uplands. The University of Corsica is situated in Corte, so the city remains at the centre of Corsican **culture**. If you visit Corte, go and see the 15th-century fortress built into the side of the cliffs. If you feel like shopping, head to the Cours Paoli. There are plenty of little shops to keep you entertained.

Ajaccio, in southern Corsica, may be the most famous city on the island. It is the birthplace of the most famous Corsican, Napoleon Bonaparte. One thing is certain: if you visit Ajaccio, you will not forget he was born here. Streets, towers and **shrines** are all named after Napoleon. Of course, that is one of the best reasons to visit Ajaccio. You can learn all about France's most famous dictator and his place in history by visiting his childhood home and the Napoleon Museum. Then you can take a break to enjoy napoleon pastries on one of Ajaccio's busiest streets – the Cours Napoleon.

▼ NAPOLEON PASTRY

Corsica is the birthplace of France's famous emperor, Napoleon Bonaparte. This cake is called a napoleon.

FASCINATING FACT

Napoleon...great leader or great cake? The answer is both. Why is there a cake called a napoleon? Rumour has it that this puff pastry was created by a Danish royal pastry chef. He invented it in the 1800s to honour the French leader Napoleon Bonaparte.

Holidays

The French people celebrate many national and religious holidays. Bastille Day on 14 July, is the most significant national holiday. It celebrates the beginning of the French Revolution in 1789. Armistice Day, or Remembrance Day, is on 11 November. It honours French soldiers, especially those who fought in World Wars I and II. May Day on 1 May is also important. May Day honours French workers.

Many of the major holidays in France are Christian. The most important is Christmas (or Nöel in French). Nöel celebrates the birth of Jesus. Easter (Pâques) is another important religious holiday in France. It commemorates Jesus' death and resurrection.

▲ **BASTILLE DAY PARADE**
On Bastille Day there are lots of parades with music, uniforms and French flags.

Learning the language

English	French	How to say it
Hello	Bonjour	bon-JHOOR
Goodbye	Au revoir	OH rev-WAHR
How are you	Comment allez-vous?	ko-MOT AH-lay VOO
My name is	Je m'appelle	JHEH mah-PELL
Please	S'il vous plait	SEE VOO PLAY
Thank you	Merci	MEHR-see
Excuse me	Excusez-moi	ek-SKYOO-say MWAH

Quick facts

France

Capital
Paris

Borders
English Channel (N)
Belgium, Luxembourg,
Germany, Switzerland,
Italy (E), Spain, Monaco,
Mediterranean Sea (S), Atlantic
Ocean (W)

Area
543,965 sq km
(210,026 sq miles)

Population
59,765,983

Largest cities
Paris (2,113,000
people)
Marseilles (815,000)
Lyons (444,000)
Toulouse (406,000)

▼ Main religious groups

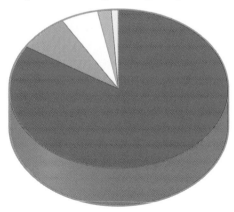

Roman Catholic 84%
Muslim 7.5%
Other 5.5%
Protestant 2%
Jewish 1%

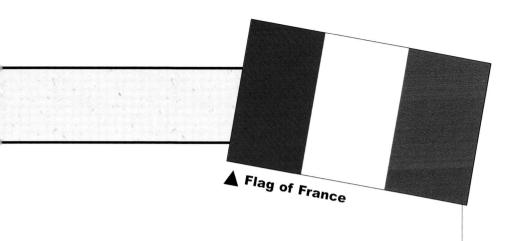

▲ Flag of France

Coastline ▶
3427 km (2130 miles)

Longest river
Loire
1020 km (634 miles)

Literacy rate
99% of all French
people can read

Major industries
Steel, machinery,
chemicals, cars

**Main crops and
livestock**
Cereals, sugarbeet,
potatoes, wine grapes,
cattle, fish

Natural resources
Coal, iron ore, bauxite,
fish, timber

◀ **Monetary unit**
Euro

People to know

◄ Sophie Marceau

Sophie Marceau was born in Paris, in 1966. She started acting at the age of fourteen and became very popular with her first film. Born Sophie Maupu, she changed her name to Marceau just before the release of her first runaway French hit, *La Boum*. Sophie has worked with Mel Gibson, Gerard Depardieu, Pierce Brosnan and other famous film stars.

Jacques Cousteau ►

Jacques Cousteau amazed the world with his underwater adventures. He brought the undersea world to television with specially built cameras and boats. He also invented the scuba tank for breathing under water.

◄ Joan of Arc

One of the most famous French people, Joan of Arc helped defend France against the English. The English eventually captured her and burnt her at the stake in 1431. She died when she was only nineteen years old.

More to read

Do you want to know more about France? Take a look at the books below.

Take your camera to France, Ted Park.
  (Raintree, 2003)
Lots of excellent photos and plenty of information to help you plan your trip to France.

Step into France, Fred Martin.
  (Heinemann Library, 1998)
Discover what life in France is like including what the people eat, where they go shopping and what games they play.

Next Stop France, Fred Martin.
    (Heinemann Library, 1998)
Take a tour of France and understand its past and present. Learn what France is really like – the land, the weather, the animals and the people.

Turning Points in History: Fall of the Bastille, Stewart Ross
    (Heinemann Library, 2001)
Delve into the very nature of history and learn about the key events, the cause and the effect of this important occasion in French history.

Nations of the World: France, Richard Ingham.
  (Raintree, 2003)
  Explore the history, economy, geography and culture of France in depth, and get real feel for the country.

Glossary

alliance agreement to work together

ancestor person's older relative who was alive a long time ago

chandelier large, ornate hanging light fixture

climate type of weather in a place

colony territory settled in or ruled by people from a state abroad or overseas

commemorate do something special to honour someone or something

culture way of life of a particular society

décor style used to decorate a room or space

democracy form of government in which the people vote for their officials

dynasty series of rulers from the same family

economic depression period of time when businesses do badly and people cannot make enough money

equator imaginary line around the middle of the Earth, halfway between the North and South poles

export send products to another country for trade or sale

fertile good for growing crops

foreign from another country

gourmet especially delicious, carefully prepared food

guillotine (GILL-oh-teen) machine used during the French Revolution to chop off a person's head

Impressionism style of painting in which the artist shows how the subject looks at a certain moment

independent when a country is self governing

invasion when people from one country enter another country by force

luxury something bought for pleasure and not out of need

monk man who lives away from society and devotes his life to his religion

natural resource property of the land, such as trees, minerals and water that occur naturally and can be used by humans

Nazi a member of the National Socialist German Workers' party, which had extreme racist and authoritarian policies

nutrient substance in food that is used by plants and animals for growth

port city where ships can safely dock to load and unload cargo

Realism a style in art and literature that aims to present things as they really are

revolution overthrow of a government by the people

shrine building or monument that is considered sacred or holy

stable unchanging

temperate describes a climate with mild temperatures

vegetation plant life

Index

DUDLEY SCHOOLS LIBRARY
AND INFORMATION SERVICE

Schools Library and Information Services

S00000650914

world tour
Australia

LEIGH ANN COBB

www.raintreepublishers.co.uk

Visit our website to find out more information about Raintree books.

To order:
☎ Phone 44 (0) 1865 888112
▤ Send a fax to 44 (0) 1865 314091
▥ Visit the Raintree Bookshop at **www.raintreepublishers.co.uk** to browse our catalogue and order online.

First published in Great Britain by Raintree Publishers, Halley Court, Jordan Hill, Oxford, OX2 8EJ, part of Harcourt Education.
Raintree is a registered trademark of Harcourt Education Ltd.

© Harcourt Education Ltd 2003
The moral right of the proprieter has been asserted.

All rights reserved. No part of this publication may be reproduced, stored in a retrieval system, or transmitted in any form or by any means, electronic, mechanical, photocopying, recording, or otherwise, without either the prior written permission of the publishers or a licence permitting restricted copying in the United Kingdom issued by the Copyright Licensing Agency Ltd, 90 Tottenham Court Road, London W1T 4LP (www.cla.co.uk).

Editorial: Sally Knowles
Cover Design: Peter Bailey and Michelle Lisseter
Production: Jonathan Smith

Printed and bound in China and Hong Kong by South China Printing Company

ISBN 1 844 21310 2
07 06 05 04 03
10 9 8 7 6 5 4 3 2 1

British Library Cataloguing in Publication Data
Cobb, Leigh Anne
Australia (World tour)
994
A full catalogue for this book is available from the British Library

Acknowledgements
The publishers would like to thank the following for permission to reproduce photographs: p.**5** ©M. Harvey/DRK Photo; p.**7** ©Charles Lenars/CORBIS; p.**8** ©Bob & Suzanne Clemenz; p.**15b** ©Joe McDonald/CORBIS; p.**19** ©Ron Dorman/Superstock; p.**21b** ©Jeffry L. Rotman/AGPix; p.**23** ©Bill Bachman; p.**24a** ©Don Pitcher; p.**24b** ©John W. Banagan/Getty Images; p.**27b** ©Siegfried Tauquer/eStock Photo; p.**28** ©Penny Tweedie/CORBIS; p.**29** ©Don Pitcher; p.**31a** ©Bill Bachman; p.**33** ©Paul Chesley/Getty Images; p.**34** ©Michael Freeman/CORBIS; p.**35** ©Foodpix; p.**37a** ©Victoria Dock/Trip/Eric Smith; p.**37b** ©Peter Mead/Tom Stack & Associates; p.**40** ©Trip/Eric Smith; p.**42** ©Ron Dorman/Superstock; p. **44a** ©CORBIS; p.**44b** ©Rufus F. Folkks/CORBIS; p.**44c** ©Jerry Lampen/CORBIS.

Additional Photography by Corbis Royalty Free, Comstock Royalty Free, Getty Images Royalty Free PhotoDisc, and the Steck-Vaughn Collection.

Cover photography: Background: Getty Images/Taxi/Terry Qing. Foreground: Getty Images/Stone/Paul Chesley

Every effort has been made to contact copyright holders of any material reproduced in this book. Any omissions will be rectified in subsequent printing if notice is given to the publishers.

DUDLEY PUBLIC LIBRARY

-46682

650914   SCH

J919.4